# The Joseph Principle

"The Answer to Economic Crisis"

Author:
Donald J. McClintock

The opinions expressed in this manuscript are solely the opinions of the author and do not represent the opinions or thoughts of the publisher. The author has represented and warranted full ownership and/or legal right to publish all the materials in this book.

The Joseph Principle
"The Answer to Economic Crisis"
All Rights Reserved.
Copyright © 2014 Donald J. McClintock
v3.0

Cover Photo © 2014 Donald J. McClintock. All rights reserved - used with permission.

This book may not be reproduced, transmitted, or stored in whole or in part by any means, including graphic, electronic, or mechanical without the express written consent of the publisher except in the case of brief quotations embodied in critical articles and reviews.

Outskirts Press, Inc.
http://www.outskirtspress.com

ISBN: 978-1-4787-0123-1

Outskirts Press and the "OP" logo are trademarks belonging to Outskirts Press, Inc.

PRINTED IN THE UNITED STATES OF AMERICA

# Reviewed By:

"Pastor Don in his first book "The Joseph Principle" has captured the common sense approach of the Gospel of the Kingdom to position the citizens of the Kingdom of God to have influence and dominion in every sphere of humanity. And through relationship and divine connection, offer solutions that facilitate the wealth management and transfer necessary to protect and insure the stability of a nation and a people whose hearts and lives are turned towards HIM!"

Bishop E. L. Warren
International Network of Affiliate Ministries
Quincy, IL

"There are those who write books but "The Joseph Principle" is a book written with undying passion, extreme purpose, and Kingdom principles that will challenge your thinking demanding a change that will bring you hope and an intended future for you, your family, people and nation."

Pastor Zack Strong
Christ Church of the Heartland
Cape Girardeau, MO

"Don McClintock is a unique and refreshing voice in the Body of Christ today. He speaks and writes with an anointed Kingdom mixture of anointing and intelligence.

His ability to blend relationship with the King with knowledge and expertise in Kingdom principles will inspire, inform, motivate and accelerate you into your next season of productivity.

His warnings, revelations and solutions are poignant and relevant to today with its multiple challenges.

Don McClintock's writing will be a Kingdom source of problem solving in your life."

Dr. Mike Brown
Strength & Wisdom Ministries
Branson, MO

*Dedications*

*Without the support and loving belief of the most precious and inspiring person I know, I would not be writing this. She is my covenant partner of wonderful and blissful 24 years of marriage. Thank you to my Brenda. I love you beyond knowing. Your belief in me has provided the catalyst to press forward even when there is a plate full of assignments. You truly are a gift from God in my life. "Together forever."*

*A special thank you to my children: Crystal, David, and Brittany for allowing me the time to study, write and think. I love you guys. You are the best that a daddy could ask for.*

*Thanks to all those who have believed in what God has called me to do. Thank you to the loving congregation of Eagle Heights Worship Center. It is a privilege to pastor you and your families.*

*Thank you to such a prolific close friend for the value he is in my life, Bishop Henry Phillips. Bishop and his gifted wife, Dr. Patricia, have wisely imparted into our lives. They pastor Power of Change Christian Center in Cahokia, IL.*

*Thank you to my father, Dr. Don McClintock, whom I love deeply for his encouragement of me in school and ministry.*

*In memory of my Mother, Marge, for her impact in my life through music, arts, and writing. She will be missed. I know that you would be proud.*

*In memory of Apostle Fred Pine, my father-in-law, and the one who would tell me like it was as he saw it. His heart was huge and I'm blessed to have known him. Heaven's gain is our loss.*

*To very special women, Mama Char and Mama Pine (Barbara); they sow love in so many different ways. These are the wonderful grandmas of our children.*

*A special dedication to the minister whose obedience to the Holy Spirit unlocked my feet- Pastor Zack Strong - thank you. Pastor Zack and his good wife, Diane, pastor Christ Church of the Heartland in Cape Girardeau, MO.*

*A special mention of the minister that prophesied that "books were in me"- love you to Prophet Sam Woods from Living Waters Lighthouse in Oklahoma City, OK.*

*To Jason & Lolita Bear for their help in editing and serving, thank you guys.*

*To John Renfro for an awesome graphic design of my cover; special gratitude.*

*To my Heavenly Father for the gift to pen words of inspiration and thought.*

# Table of Contents

Foreword ................................................................... ix
Preface ..................................................................... xi
Introduction............................................................ xv
The Awakening of Leaders to a Crisis ...................... 1
The Proper Diagnosis and Accurate Prediction ........ 7
The Right Leaders in Authority–Lead Change ........ 12
The Abundant Years – The Now Preparation ........... 17
The Lean Years – The Storm Hits ........................... 24
The Exchange – The Price of the Unprepared ......... 28
The Results are "In" ................................................ 33
The Other Side of the Crisis – The New Beginning . 37
Epilogue ................................................................. 41
Call to Action ......................................................... 41
References Recommended ..................................... 56
Bibliography ........................................................... 57
Advertisements & Products .................................... 59
Contact Information................................................ 60
Author's Short Biography ....................................... 61

# Foreword

"Rarely do you find an author who is able to write like an ancient scribe and as a modern business guru at the same time. In a world filled with financial books presenting dated formulas for success, leaving hundreds and thousands of people disenfranchised with high hopes but very little results, I am resolved that this book steps away from that presentation to provide a fresh, relevant and relatable approach to finance.

Today, people are seeking principles that transcend pop culture success that only lasts for a moment. Knowing what to do or who to trust with money matters is paramount in today's economic structure. If there was ever a time we need a Joseph found in scripture to provide a foolproof remedy that will empower you with ideology for thriving in today's economic shifts. It is now.

In this book, "The Joseph Principle", Don McClintock reveals the preparation of a man that would have to lead nations to economic stability in difficult times. The story of Joseph will not only fascinate you with the similarities of today's social crisis and how short term planning and a lack of integrity can cost you everything, it will literally teach you Economics 101. This book is sure to transform your mind about the use of your resources as its builds from chapter to chapter.

I'm excited that Don McClintock decided to take this material one step further by offering you some suggested investments and entrepreneurial pursuits, relevant for today.

Whether you need to reposition yourself for financial success or build a new foundation altogether, this book is sure to develop the framework needed to move you in the right direction. It is my hope that you will experience God's abundance as you read" The Joseph Principle"."

Bishop – Dr. Henry Phillips

Ecclesia Covenant Fellowship International, Presiding Prelate

Power of Change Christian Center, Cahokia, IL

# Preface

Inspired and intrigued by the Joseph story in the Bible plus my search for answers that would help so many people survive a downdraft of the economy not seen since the Great Depression, I reveal my findings of a life saving prototype that just could be the sound solution to what would otherwise be a profound disaster for millions.

I believe that in reading "The Joseph Principle", every reader will not only understand the coming monetary and economical crisis, but also find common sense applicable steps to assuring that their future is not as stressful as could be without this important and vital insight.

After writing papers on the Financial Crisis of 2008, its causes and effects, I have spent many hours both in research and contemplation that lead me to this book.

As I am writing this book, we are still stuck in a financial crisis prolonged by incompetence, political power structures, and an injection of trillions of dollars in debt. High unemployment and the possible dethroning of the U.S. dollar as the World Reserve Currency could add to the stress in the system.

Inflation is accelerating in food, materials, energy, and other goods. This is the stated strategy of the Federal Reserve designed to lift us out of the recession we were sunk into by immoral greed sanctioned by our Congress in policy, our Federal Reserve in monetary policy, and our government in regulations that contributed to the bubble burst.

It is mind boggling to think of over $16.9 trillion dollars of debt and growing.* To those that don't know, that's a debt of approximately $53,428.00 (est.) for every American.* This is how much each and every American now owes thanks to our elected officials in Washington D.C. (especially those who have served from four to thirty years).

Finally, there is talk of doing something. We need more than talk. We cannot afford to stand by and trust our government to solve these humungous problems.

There are steps that we can take as individuals to insure our future. Action is needed now rather than later. The deep sense of entitlement is growing and is standing in the way of progressing to an answer.

The premise for this book is to bring out an ancient principle that saved two nations from destruction and see how the wisdom of that event can be applied to help solve our present day dilemma.

It could be that history is set to repeat itself. It is my goal to aid every reader in preparation for the near future. We are not insulated from the effects of the decisions of our leaders. Ignorance is no longer an excuse reports the IRS, neither is it a viable excuse now. The answer is within our grasp. Let's embrace it.

# Introduction

The Story of Joseph is an in depth study of how to hold on to the gift of a dream given, even when faced with intense challenges and social rejection. All of the challenges aid in the development of his character and the breadth of his ability for heavy weighted responsibility.

The plan that he revealed to the Pharaoh of Egypt is what I have named "The Joseph Principle". We will look carefully into his encounter with government leadership, the process of the plan and its results. Embedded in this experience is an answer that can be applied in periods of economic difficulty.

It is clear that we presently need more self-motivated individuals to respond in a Joseph DNA. We cannot afford to be short of Josephs in our society. There must be some "leaders- in- the- making" strangely obscure to the high profile public that will rise to the forefront and answer the call of the Dream.

It is important that every reader educate themselves in these subjects. Ignorance is not bliss; rather it is easily controlled and manipulated. Informed persons ask the questions that bring out the appropriate accountability needed to guard our freedom and liberty.

It is clear that experience and education must cover the following: proper purpose of life, spirituality, economics, money, employment position, and disciplined work ethic. Learned knowledge and wisdom in each are crucial in application of adequate handling of any real crisis.

There will be those who sense the urgency and with a rational plan prepare for that which could arise. This is risk management. If nothing happens great or something does happen, one is prepared. For this same reason we purchase insurance of all sorts to manage risk.

There will be those who choose to ignore the warning and then pay the high cost of loss by taking all of the risk upon themselves. Given this, without preparation it would mean certain catastrophe at the survival level. Why not save for a rainy day?

Keep the budget modest and it will make the good times better and the bad times not so painful. It is sound advice for one to have a store for the winter. It is sound advice for one to save and invest for retirement. It is sound advice to put away for the children's college fund. It is sound advice to prepare for that which is looming over our economy.

This is a saver's investor mentality, not the spender/debtor mentality. A saver can end up the owner. The debtor ends up having spent their future too far in advance. The saver's mentality is the slower, calculated, and simpler life style. It is not one that believes everything is owed to them, but rather that one can work, save, and invest to secure their future.

Joseph was one who would rise to the top no matter what position he was placed in. When allowed to operate his skills, he would find favor with his supervisors. His skills in administration and finance brought much prosperity to those he worked for.

Joseph didn't act as if all he had to do was show up to get paid. He took whatever task and responsibilities given to him as serious business. His diligence and accuracy paid off for him in time. He showed great patience and restraint, but when all was said and done, Joseph was again at the top and being compensated quite well.

From age 17, Joseph spent thirteen years in great challenges, fourteen years working the plan, and fifty-six years living wealthy and enjoying life to the fullest. Contrary to our system now where the working years are fifty and the enjoyment years are fifteen, obscurely opposite.

Joseph was compensated for the answer to a crisis that saved the lives and welfare of tens of thousands of people. He was given the task of a lifetime and answered the call with character and integrity both essential to the survival of those who were counting on him for the provision that he directly oversaw. He was not busy taking extended coffee breaks and ordering extra donuts. Joseph input the discipline necessary to accomplish the task with excellence.

We find the recorded account in the Book of *Genesis chapters 39-50*.

We'll select key portions of this account to reveal the plan that saved two nations, known as "The Joseph Principle". If each reader begins to implement the principles revealed as they read, you will be well on your way to being prepared. Time is of the essence in this matter.

# 1

# The Awakening of Leaders to a Crisis

QUOTE:
"ONE OF THE TRUE TESTS OF LEADERSHIP IS THE ABILITY TO RECOGNIZE A PROBLEM BEFORE IT BECOMES AN EMERGENCY."
ARNOLD H. GLASOW

Principle:
"Leaders are by nature of character forward looking visionaries and must discern both good and bad."

**AN AWAKENED LEADER** is more than just an informed bureaucrat with a reelection agenda. To have some advance notice that a crisis is coming over the horizon can be taken several ways: 1) ignore the warning and hope it never materializes, 2) use the warning to spin an agenda, 3) discredit the source of the warning, or 4) take the warning to heart and develop a plan to either avert the crisis or handle it with competence and effectiveness.

Those leaders that are not awakened will procrastinate because the threat or peril is not presently exploding in their faces. Those that are awakened begin to take appropriate action in advance of the peril or crisis even in the face of public response that may need to be educated to the facts that brought their leaders to make the decision to act.

It requires more than personality and a large reelection fund to produce a qualified and effectual leader. The leader of Egypt at the time of this account was Pharaoh, whose power was derived from the consent of lords and princes plus his army and his country's religious beliefs. Pharaoh had no clue of the pending crisis waiting in his country's future until he had two dreams that trouble him to his core.

He was so troubled that he called all of his advisors and counselors for their interpretation of the dreams. All of them failed to bring any interpretation. All would have been lost had not a government employee, the King's butler, asked to speak up and give a recommendation for a man that could give interpretation to the troubling dreams.

Once awakened, Pharaoh would not stop until this

matter had been properly investigated and a satisfactory answer acquired. He permitted and arranged an audience with the man recommended to him.

What do you do as a leader who is disturbed by the information that you are now aware of and no one in your administration has the accurate details that you require in order to make an executive decision that will impact all of those who are under your supervision?

Many leaders are snared in the trap of sameness and the temptation to declare normalcy. They surround themselves with those who cannot speak from a clear perspective or are merely "yes" persons to the leader's authority for self-benefit. The effect that power and influence has not only upon followers, but also on the leaders is simply intoxicating to a majority of those who come to that position of prestige.

Pharaoh turned to a thirty year old criminal non-national in his investigation based upon the verbal and personal referral of his royal butler and cupbearer.

His royal butler told the king of his encounter with the slave outcast. He told of the accuracy of his interpretations. It was that impressive testimony that a desperate king relied on when ordering a summons of the man Joseph into the royal court to be heard by the Pharaoh.

Truly awakened leaders are willing to look beyond the "yes only" persons and the ideological clones to observe a possible solution that may not fit in the box of normal.

It is this inner fortitude that separates political-leaders from real leaders. The decision should be made by one that has looked at the possible conclusions and has forged a plan of action, then implementing such a solution so that the crisis is avoided or the impact of it lessened.

When leaders are focused on power, personal agenda, influence and position, then the well-being of the people they govern is reduced to the least possible quality that assures there will be no uprising. When great leaders rule, the guidelines are set through civility, morality, and wisdom. This model of leadership requires that the people increase in knowledge, understanding and purpose.

In any leader's lifetime of service, whether a king or an elected official, times present challenges that require their best, even beyond best. This is a stretching of thought that will heighten their level of service.

Some don't see the crisis until it is too late; others see it but tell the people there is nothing to worry about.

This is a weak and cowardice position that many take thinking that those they rule over will simply forget or are too stupid to understand.

Still others try to capitalize on a fake crisis and try to sweep under the carpet any authentic crisis. This is "agenda governance" not true principled leadership.

In being a true leader, there are decisions that require a great deal of courage and inner strength. This is especially true when many human lives are at stake. "How sad the moment of crisis;… okay let's move on now," say some. A moment of apparent realism then on to other subjects is typical of politicians who cast shadows to insure their own power. This is not the way of leadership that really cares for the lives and well-being of those under their oversight.

Only through the strong courage of those that are true can a standard of sanity and common sense bring right judgment to those who are indulgent in their own sense of pride.

When leaders are awakened, a nation hopes that they have the knowledge and the fortitude to make the right decision even though others may not comprehend the devastation that was avoided.

Revealed are great leaders who do not attempt to band-aid the crisis by only treating the symptoms with a pain killer. This only eases the suffering artificially, but still kills the patient. Cowards are those who simply try to put off into tomorrow what is necessary today.

A leader must not declare that a crisis is fixed prematurely. Attempting to quiet the awakening of others when the answer has not taken hold can weaken the resolve and through complacency leave a people vulnerable again to a disaster.

Once Pharaoh had awakened to a pending crisis, he refused to ignore it or pass it off to the next leader. He continued investigating until he had an answer that he felt confident would solve the problem of his nation starving to death. When presented a plan, he was courageous and enacted the authority to put the plan into action.

It is that kind of courage needed today to overt crisis and minimize human suffering that could be magnified by the highly possible and predicted crisis.

The most courageous leaders must be able to withstand pressure from critics and overcome the debate with detailed plan to solve the crisis. In the story, there is a timetable of seven good years and seven famine years.

In a present time crisis, solutions must work in four years or a total political swing of control will occur at the voting booth. A great leader would have to lay his re-election hopes and want for power down at the feet of integrity and responsibility.

If millions are aware of the impending crisis and given a decisive plan to avert it, they can be a powerful support for the leader to achieve the solutions needed. Sadly, there are too many millions that only see in the small world of their own pride of life. They live in the world of free assistance and this clouds their judgment to any change other than "more of the same."

This leaves the crisis to happen and the clean-up be the answer. Destruction is far too expensive when the cost is human lives. Leaders awake!

# 2 | The Proper Diagnosis and Accurate Prediction

QUOTE:
"WHEN TROUBLE ARISES AND THINGS LOOK BAD, THERE IS ALWAYS ONE INDIVIDUAL WHO PERCEIVES A SOLUTION AND IS WILLING TO TAKE COMMAND."
        DAVE BARRY

Principle:
"Perception, preparation and problem solving are crucial leadership skills."

**WITHOUT A PURPOSED** perception of one's future, a person will abandon discipline and/or pursue the wrong process that will result in devastation, like an old barn slowly falling down one board at a time. This does not need to happen.

A vision of accuracy and a proper diagnosis of the events ahead will aid in the avoidance of that catastrophic destruction. Even though the hard times and difficult challenges are still present and very real, equipped with the right information, understanding, and wisdom one can preserve the outcome and reduce its negative impact.

Famines were not uncommon in the ancient times. Rainfall amounts varied and were crucial to agriculture, plants, and grass for livestock, streams, etc. There were those who migrated and did not have a storage system. The city states and nations with multiple cities were more apt to have places for storage close to the market place.

The strategy of storage was one of the few successful strategies to overcome famine. One other may have been to go to war and take the harvest of others nearby. People will do strange things if they are starving. The need for fresh and/or stored food is a biological necessity.

In history, people were led to a wide variety of behaviors when facing mass starvation. The impulse to survive brings out some the irrational human side from thievery to cannibalism.

If a famine is predicted, especially one that would last seven years, there would need to be sufficient time for preparation to curb the result of those impending inhumanities.

The more accurate the prediction, the better that one can make appropriate changes to be ready and use survival techniques to outlast the famine.

Historical evidence and accounts were frequently used to make a proper diagnosis and present a prediction. The question is how far back does one go into historical data to conclude a diagnosis that will yield accuracy?

Many economists' predictions turn out to be wrong. Many statisticians and theorists can only determine a degree or level of confidence where error or chance of being wrong is stated. An accurate prediction of this magnitude is highly improbable or near impossible.

Yet, contrary to the mainstream opinion polls, someone has come to some information that diagnoses and predicts a serious problem is about to occur. Persons of renown are setting markers in the sands of time that they feel crucial to the unveiling of the crisis. They base this upon the facts, symptoms, and laws of absolute truth.

Put it all together and one finds the pieces have formed a picture that must be acted upon and not allowed to run its course without some means of attempted cure.

Joseph not only had a track record of predicting by interpretation of dreams a potential outcome with precise accuracy, but was called upon to do the same at a national level of responsibility.

Joseph seemed the most unlikely candidate for a

leader of a nation to base such a colossal decision upon. We notice that the King's butler refers to Joseph as "a young Hebrew with us in the prison who was a slave of the Captain of the Guard." And everything happened just as he predicted. This is a stunning personal testimony of a trusted government employee.

This opened the door for Joseph's appointment with Pharaoh. This was his opportunity to shine. Joseph cleaned his appearance and walks in with dignity and honor.

Joseph presented the interpretation with such confidence and courage that all were amazed. He presented not only the crisis but also the solution and process to solve it. He then humbly gave a recommendation of the selection and appointment of a new cabinet member without the pretense that it be him.

Proper diagnosis and accurate predictions are not for the getting of attention on behalf of the predictor, but rather to reinforce that the attention of those who will be affected by such a calamity be apprehended. The preservation of lives and lifestyle are weighted a larger value than the inconvenience of upsetting the status-quo.

It may be that the status-quo is of enough excesses to provide the ingredients for a wide spread crisis, not ideological crisis. The housing trouble signs were present for two years prior to the crash of 2008, yet those who could avert the crisis and recession chose to do nothing because they were connected to the toxins that were profiting off of the excesses.

This conflict of interest and profiting of millions to

cronies taints the judgment of those officials who have the power to table all or delay any effective investigation into the validity of the prediction. This leads us to the extreme importance of not only the right predictions but the right leaders.

# 3

# The Right Leaders in Authority-Lead Change

QUOTE:
"NEARLY ALL MEN CAN STAND ADVERSITY, BUT IF YOU WANT TO TEST A MAN'S CHARACTER, GIVE HIM POWER."
       ABRAHAM LINCOLN

Principle:
*"When the righteous are in authority, the people rejoice."*
       *Proverb*

**IT IS VITALLY** important to have the right people in leadership. Those whose entire role is to both serve and lead in a manner that not only accomplished the tasks and responsibilities of the job with competence and accuracy, but also brings about positive change that will set a course for hopefully generations to come.

It is these that through character and wisdom leave a legacy that brings about preservation of life and/or an innovation that fuels creative thinking and investor partnering. They hold high the standard of the freedom of the individual to choose within a framework governed by peace.

Joseph was selected for the high government position and task fulfillment not by political favor or by resume, but by the qualifications of wisdom, protocol, and divine understanding of how to complete the assignment given.

"A God given dream defines you, motivates you, reveals your purpose, and confirms you," a quote by Pastor Zack Strong.

The most advanced leaders have a vision or dream that governs their actions. Joseph is elevated to a high government position, likened to the Chief Operating Officer over agriculture and commerce. He is given the latitude and power to implement whatever resources needed to preserve a nation over a fourteen year timeframe. This is the biggest undertaking of his life.

Joseph had an insight and interpretation to the King's dream that no one else possessed. He would work faithfully and consistently for nine of the fourteen years before he saw his dreams manifest before his eyes.

It is this new career path that leads to the fulfillment of that which is divinely given. It is this synergy of both that brings the passion and expression of courage in the latter five years of the assignment. A real good leader not only sells the plan and vision to others, but has the inner courage and belief to take the necessary risks. Joseph will take seven years building and storing for the latter seven years of famine. He stayed the course.

A quality leader should be examined by the influences of their past. Leaders are not born as leaders; there is a process both inward and outward. To understand the true destination of their leadership skills, we must look at the DNA of the person.

Each individual will show signs of the influences that directly impact their thought processes. The mentors in their life will have provided an adjustment one way or another. It is those associations that give some analysis as to the type of leader that each will become.

What is in them will be the substance that flows out of their efforts and purposes. What flows from them will also be prevalent on them and all around them. The atmosphere that they set for their environment will yield huge clues as to the essence of that leader.

Just because one is good looking or a great orator doesn't make them a leader that history will look back on and record that they led with an exemplary manner and showed extraordinary courage in the toughest times.

Two questions asked too late are: "What did they leave behind after they were gone" and "what did they do meaningful while they had the opportunity?" Both questions are time sensitive and are not predictors but rather rear view indicators.

The right leaders should not be chosen because of vanity and prepared speeches. It used to be that leaders were selected by the things that had accomplished; now you are a great candidate for leadership if you have done nothing.

History shows us many leaders. Some good and wise, others ruled by force. John Maxwell writes,

"Leadership is influence." That seems to be the simplest definition, but leaves out what type of influence and whether they are the right leaders.

Influence is present where one has submitted to receive its instruction. It is preferred that influence come and be received through civility, morality, and wisdom. Oddly, some will refuse the very influence that will help them.

The right leaders help to give a framework that will provide the judicial guide for their people to develop and grow, learn and prosper, live and enjoy life. When the right leaders are in authority, the people live well and have healthy lives. Leadership doesn't let an individual do whatever they want to do without teaching them the guide patterned for civility, morality, and wisdom.

To the chaotic, any guide or law would seem an intrusion into individual freedom, but for a balance that still rewards personal achievement, laws must be patterned. The right leadership will give opportunity to all within that structure of law. The choice will be given after the education is adequate to the boundaries and the potential.

Not lending to class warfare, the right leaders in authority show others, not dictate, the path that leads to high achievement and reward.

This means the integral use of authority is entrusted and then delegated.

Delegation is not reward for cronyism, but is afforded to qualified and capable leadership to enhance the quality and effectiveness of head leader's vision.

All delegated authority must adhere to the guidelines set before them and not supersede the boundaries of authority given.

It is Joseph's integrity, understanding, wisdom, and vision casting that are part of his resume. Pharaoh uses this, the report of his butler, and the evidence that Joseph had the real spirit of God in him to lead him. All of these are important to revealing those qualified for authority over others to lead in a manner that preserves life and the quality of life.

The right leaders do not manifest the actions of revenge upon those that have mistreated them before. Justice is allowed to perform her work. Joseph did not enact revenge toward his brethren but tested them.

Neither did he exact power to get even with Potipher's wife for the false accusation and prison time served because of the injustice.

When in authority, none of his abusers dare continue the same line of persecution upon him.

The right leaders will focus their careers upon the fair enrichment of all. They will reward those that participate in the accomplishment of that life-preserving vision.

The question is: "Where do we find such leadership in the making in the land today that will follow those qualities and not be corrupted by the power and fortune that leading may provide?"

Where do we find those leaders that believe that they should lead in accordance with our Constitution, the framework of our Founding Fathers?

# 4

# The Abundant Years - The Now Preparation

*Quote:*
*"The empowerment of great leadership is embodied in these elements: Integrity, truth, courage, discernment, and confidence of others."*
       *Donald J. McClintock*

Principle:
"Make you budget lean and effective; then the bad years are not as bad and the good years are even better."
       *Donald J. McClintock*

**WHEN THERE IS** an envelope of time prior to a possible or certain crisis, one must utilize those moments to begin preparation. This is not crying wolf, when none is present. This is reading the signs that present themselves by circumstances or by people of understanding. Preparation is a more viable course of action than sudden exposure to the incident.

To many times the abundant years are used for excessive spending and consumption with very little being actually stored, saved, or invested in an asset that produces. It becomes a literal "feast or famine"-"boom or bust" mentality. Then there are those to nibble at sowing for the future. They save for half of a rainy day.

The years where plenty is enjoyed are the perfect target for putting away a portion of the excess for a planned purpose. Potato farmers have learned that if everyone goes to market at the same time, the price will decrease because of plentiful supply and then increase sharply after harvest is far past.

The wise have learned new storage techniques in order to bring their harvest to market at different times and securing a stable and higher price for the entire harvest. Storage sends harvest into the future while spending on credit sends payments into the future at a higher total cost depleting the harvest. Some might say that sending the harvest into the future will secure a time where there is no incentive to sow for a future harvest. If there is that much harvest stored for your future, could that be called, "real retirement" or "financial independence"?

Joseph's plan was to subsidize the agricultural growth cycle of 20% of all the fertile land in Egypt either by 1/5 of the land or 1/5 of the produce of all the land. He then organized the building of storage units in all the major cities in Egypt. He then accounted for the harvest of grain from that land for seven bumper crop years until the count was beyond counting.

The plan was to have enough stored to feed all of Egypt for seven years and have enough seed to plant after the famine was over.

From the account, there seems to be enough supply to transact some grain commerce with the immediate surrounding areas that were also affected by the famine.

The logistics of this undertaking required frequent trips to those cities where building projects were being constructed. The economy was booming.

Food was plenteous. Animals were fat and healthy. Jobs were paying for qualified workers. Agriculture and construction were celebrating all time highs in production. Business was good, and no doubt the government coffers were being replenished from the economic up cycle.

Government spending was for productive business applications. Thanks to the accurate predictions of Joseph they were ahead of the cycle, not behind the curve.

The target of storage was food and for very good reasons. After many congressional reports, it was concluded that what most people have need of during a famine is "FOOD."

People and livestock would need food. Why not gold? You can't eat gold. If the food runs out, the gold will be useless. If we reversed our subsidies so that farmers would plant more land with crops, then store 20% of all they produce as payment on the subsidy, we would have an enormous supply to feed those who may be in a famine at a market price relevant to their location.

Here food supply would be assured and the prices be balanced by a brisk export market. Then the farmers could let the land rest in a rotation of fields one year out of seven to replenish the ground with natural nitrogen.

Joseph's department of government took up the surplus of the excessive abundance out of the system keeping the market from plummeting to all time lows agriculturally. The cost of food and feed went down and freed up the accumulation of monies, precious metals and livestock.

Preparation may have seemed a waste of time and energy in those first seven years of enormous plenty. Many did not take notice of what was happening in their cities or they figured out that the government was storing for the future so they didn't have to.

The human ignorance factor of short term planning caught many. Some were just too optimistic thinking that the abundant years would go on forever. Whatever the reason, the plan of Joseph worked because the people were not prepared for the last seven years.

The people had consumed the majority of their wealth and not stored. They did not follow the example of the leaders who had the forethought and risk management skills to operate a plan to the contrary of the economic season.

They didn't mind paying 20% of their grain when their harvest was up to seven times the usual harvest. The gathering of the grain was true asset accumulation by a government entity. Notice that they didn't give it away to the unemployed as welfare.

They employed all able bodied persons in the economy either by government or by private sector.

The grain storage had several different applications: 1) food supply, 2) feed supply, 3) seed supply, 4) trade value in time of shortage.

Given the climate of the region, storage life was elongated. Some (lotus) seed found in a tomb of one of the Pharaohs sprouted after being stored dormant for centuries as reported by the International Society of Environmental Botanists in January of 2000.

Even though there is a standing need for preparation, many look back at one or more years of success and forget about the certainty that a change is around the corner. This "keep a good thing going without consequence" mentality is the very thing that causes the majority of those momentarily winning at the casino to bet everything and lose it all.

This overwhelming sediment for a continued winning streak that defies all odds of probability is the attitude that professionals monitor on Wall Street to determine when a down cycle or bubble bursting is about to occur.

Where there are multiple possible outcomes, there will be a change in outcome eventually. Isn't it strange that the very ones who have the advantage of choice refuse to acknowledge that there may be a different outcome than the one they have chosen?

The lack of preparation will certainly bring about the result of total devastation. When one does not have a plan that prepares for the unusual, then the unusual prepares to include one without consent. It is in these moments that a person realizes that ignorance is not bliss.

A book of the ages quotes, "When there is plenty and a bountiful supply, forget not the one who gives you the power to get wealth." When people are satisfied and their belly is full, complacency comes and avarice springs up from the irreverent dishonor of unthankfulness.

When times turn tough, it will be one's preparation that is the supply for which one counts to survive. The ideology of consuming everything now, leaves one lacking anything to consume in the time of trouble.

The ones who have the forethought to anticipate a potential problem that the system and the supply will be scarce in the immediate future, they will take the risk to be rewarded with the wealth. These are the ones who being odd and outcast, will provide the leadership that solves a societal challenge.

The fields are full for seven years of bumper harvests. The market is full of food. The cattle are fat and meat is plentiful. It is in these good times that the temptation to become complacent comes. After several abundant years back to back, there is the tendency to reset the abundance as the normal standard. This thinking of course will make any disruption in the abundance an even harder challenge.

These abundant years were filled with employment by the Egyptian government to build storehouses and employ those that would be storehouse workers and counters of grain. They gathered until the grain was numbered beyond contemplating. The years of abundance had been stored for the next years of famine.

# 5

# The Lean Years – The Storm Hits

*Quote:*
*"The ultimate measure of a man is not where he stands in moments of comfort, but where he stands at times of challenge and controversy."*
    Dr. Martin Luther King, Jr.

Principle:
"The courage to have prepared ahead will serve to comfort in time of trouble and lack."
    Donald J. McClintock

**WHEN THE SEVEN** years of superabundance had concluded, the next year had totally different results. Rainfall had changed and so had the yield for the crops. The famine had begun, but no doubt many did not realize that it would last the entire seven years as predicted.

The grass was lean. The harvest of grain was unproductive. Those who had any stored began to use their reserves. The famine strengthened throughout the immediate region from Libya to the Negev and south to the mountains of Cush in southern Egypt. After personal supplies were depleted, many from surrounding lands came to buy grain in Egypt.

From the historic account given, many began to cry for food in the end of the first year and the beginning of the second year. Personal and family reserves were depleted even though all had seven awesome years of abundance. It is evident that many lived on the assumption that plenty means more to eat but not store.

It is this state of normalcy that crept up upon the people and influenced them not to store for the future.

According to the biblical account, the money system beyond barter in Egypt began to fail. The standard for most goods was payment in gold, silver, copper or spices unless they could barter for trade. Much of the gold was reserved for the wealthy lords and kings. Most who traded with such used the latter three silver, copper, or spices.

When they had no food, Joseph sold to them for their money. It didn't take long for the copper and silver to grow lean as well as storage supplies had. As the money ran out Joseph sold to them in exchange for their cattle and other livestock. Soon that means of exchange was exhausted and land became the means of negotiation.

This is an *example* of government rationing at set prices. This is usually a control mechanism used when supply and demand breaks down. Use of this control is to ensure stability and avoid soaring food prices that no one can conceivably pay. A good government will not let their people starve.

When all the land was bought up and since the famine lingered on, the citizens of Egypt's providences and cities sold themselves as servants to Pharaoh. Then all of the citizens were moved to the cities until time of the famine had passed.

Isn't it strange what hunger will cause one to do to survive?

It was reported that much of the riots in the Middle East were caused by food prices spiking, unemployment shooting up, and apparent disparity between the wealthy especially government and the working class.

Joseph feeds the nations during the seven years of famine. After all is sold and there is nothing else left, he starts a "Feed-for-Work" program. This enables the people to have joint venture with government.

In leasing and producing food from the land, the original share tax of twenty percent is implemented to replenish supplies and store for future bad years. This is a good limit marker for tax rates; corporate or income not higher than 20%.

The workers keep the wheels of economy turning. When they are unemployed they can become dissatisfied and begin to get unruly through violent protests.

There will always be a risk/reward system that

promotes some to a higher level of status than others. When someone agrees to employment without ownership share, they are trading that ownership for the lesser risk and lesser reward situation. They have bartered for a higher and fire risk/reward contract.

Earn all you can, save all you can, give all you can, invest all you can; but not spend all you can and become comfortable in a box.

# 6

# The Exchange - The Price of the Unprepared

QUOTE:
"BEFORE EVERYTHING ELSE, GETTING READY IS THE SECRET TO SUCCESS."
    HENRY FORD

Principle:
"Being prepared makes going through hard times less difficult"
    Donald J. McClintock

**THERE IS A** cost to be paid for being unprepared when a risk event occurs. The cost is greater when foreknowledge of that event has not produced an urgency to act. Waiting until an event occurs to act has a much higher price attached to it.

Even if the Egyptian government did not share the plan and course predicted with the public, there should have been those who figured something was happening. When they saw the new building activity in the cities and the new grain tax being extracted from the producers either in the fields to be brought to the cities for storage or in the marketplace, there should have been those who decided to follow suit. That was a huge clue something was going on more than a government work program.

In the seven great harvest years, even with a twenty percent grain tax, there was plenty to both sell and store for possible lean years. From the account we can deduct that there were those who ignored the activity all around them and only put aside an emergency storage for about one year. That is more than a majority of Americans do presently. About 75% of Americans do not have six month's salary saved aside for emergency or for retirement.*

Many may have only put aside what history had shown by family tradition. Many may have seen the government grain storage as a proactive measure that assured them that they didn't have to do anything, because the government would take care of them.

The exchange price for unpreparedness is always of a higher cost than being prepared.

"Keep the budget low and it will make the good

times better and the hard times not as hard," spoken to me by a close friend. Great advice to follow when there is uncertainty in the future.

The challenges in life can strike at different levels at different times to different people. We are not assured that those challenges will never occur in our world of living. One great key to safety rules and plans is "preparedness." If one is not prepared one is not assured how they will react, let alone how much damage to life may occur.

Seven years is a long time to predict and prepare for seven years of severe famine.

Those occurrences may come once in a lifetime, but they do come. Nature and humanity play a key role in most occurrences. The other is disease.

When one is moderately prepared for the life's bumps in the road, then there is a certain peace that can be gained from the survival and ability to get back on course.

Sometimes, though prepared, the challenges are deeper and more intense than one planned to deal with. The valley may be dry and the mountain seemly impassable, but hope carries one on even more so with some preparedness.

It is then that one needs Divine Providence to assist beyond the scope of human activity.

Those that prepare may seem to be slower and more methodical in life by not splurging the necessities or the essentials of life for a mere moment of self-indulgence. There will be room for the finer things when preparations are completed.

It is that discipline of life and self that restrains one

from crashing and burning from greed and lust for things. There must be a higher purpose to life than self indulgence and momentary living.

In our account, many thousands were unprepared and ended up trading in all their money, animals, houses, lands and even themselves. When all was said and done, there were masses of people owned by the government.

The exchange of unpreparedness was their freedom as an individual. The price was servitude to the leadership above them. "Only if" - they hadn't consumed all the excess. "Only if" - they would have prepared.

When the light of preparedness comes on, it will determine ones outcome. They could not prepare when the famine hit. It was too late then.

So many stories try to convey this principle from the "Three Little Pigs" to "Building Your House upon the Rock" to the training of boy scouts and military. The neglect of this principle leads to the underlying horror that sixty percent of Americans are not saving sufficiently for retirement.

"Live in the moment" is true if you are reflecting upon the outcome of the future in a manner that will lead to a positive decision. Those life moment decisions are researched, informed, and then the spontaneity of the decision can be joyous. What is the end result of that decision? Decisions form our lives. Everyday those decisions construct our future.

If one is prepared and nothing happens then that one has plenty in reserve to utilize for the good of themselves and others.

If one isn't prepared, then most certainly their

lives are permanently changed and sometimes at a level that makes rebuilding a new life a huge challenge. Which would you rather be: prepared or unprepared? The choice is yours. The next one to experience a crisis may be you. Are you prepared? What price will you pay?

# 7
## The Results are "In"

QUOTE:
"WHAT YOU HONOR MOVES TOWARD YOU; WHAT YOU DISHONOR MOVES AWAY."
  DR. MIKE BROWN

Principle:
"The End of a Thing Speaks Loudly to the Authenticity of its Origin."
  Donald J. McClintock

**THE LACK OF** honor to God Almighty has severed the lines of respect for godly principles. Add the lack of partnership of a democratic republic with honest capitalism. Strip out wisdom and the end recipe is an evil system of chaos filled with greed, political force, and a self-proclaimed superiority to the wisdom of the Creator.

Allow the economy system to be a system of expanding rubber bands of falsified wealth. Allow sharks (capital cronyism) at one end and piranha (legal greed by government decree) at the other end and the result is a majority of the masses left stunned and injured by the snap of the burst of the system ("great recession").

The results are coming in. We are destroying our currency worth by increasing our debt to engulf an entire year's total output of the entire country's gross national product. We are enslaving the masses to joblessness, low pay, foreclosures, and bankruptcies. The Federal Reserve has under gird the economy by monetizing over $2 trillion in debt by buying up mortgage backed securities and will continue to buy $85 billion of that debt each month for the near future to allow banks to lend.*

Who are they going to buy those securities from? Freddie Mac, Fannie Mae & GNMA own almost 60% of all home mortgages.* Exactly! Some of the culprits involved in the bursting of the housing market bubble were from these organizations.

Monetization is exactly what will cause inflation by lowering currency and raising commodity prices making it difficult for new job creation; while they say this will help increase job creation. This false sense of securing is aiding the fiscal cliff problem because the government will not work correctly when so close to elections.

The producer price index had a bigger than expected increase; inflation in costs to producers, which may increase prices to the consumers. **The Results:** 22.6 million people unemployed or under employed; unemployment unreliable because over 8 million people have left the work force; federal deficit spending over 1 trillion a year for the last three years and projected out another 5 years; a record 43 million citizens on food stamps; plus gasoline and food prices still rising.

There are repercussions to the government holding over 60% of all mortgages and $30,000 of education debt for over 60% of college graduates. *Affordable housing & affordable education; at what cost?

The Super-wealthy are still getting wealthier, yet the current administration wants to raise taxes on those that make over $450,000 a year on their adjusted gross income. This will continue to erode the farmers and "Mom & Pop" small businesses. Where is our job creating tax reduction aid to help them add jobs? Rather, are we are increasing the load and bringing extinction to this part of the American dream?

When leaders are disposed to the same mind set that has gotten us into this economic mess, we end up patching holes while using an axe to bludgeon a new one. After many years the amount of water being taken into the ship cannot be band-aided any longer.

When we have spoiled a people to expect something for little, it is hard to change the course and retrain the masses to work hard to achieve their dreams without freebies unless there is an emergency.

If you help a butterfly out of its cocoon it will die, not being strong enough for its new environment. The same happens when one helps a baby chick exit the shell. Each must be let alone to attain the strength and determination to exit by their own power. It is crucial that they learn these skills in order to thrive in their new environment.

These are instinctive skills that come from the will to live and survive. When I speak of my fellow Americans, the instinct to live and dream can be lost when we do not have the tools to develop our God given talents and gifts. If we have the access to and the support for, then we will see an expansion of knowledge and skills amongst our citizens that catapult us ahead of the monthly and some times daily struggle to make ends meet. What's missing are the inner components of integrity, true values, and financial literacy.

Proper education economically and financially is lacking and must be fixed. Life skills are necessary to living a successful and peaceful life.

Empowering our youth to think outside of the constraints of the system, legally, and effectively, without chaos, crime, and conscientiously will take a new beginning of both thought and learning practices. The new beginning will happen by purpose and design or by anarchy and overthrow.

Seeding a restoration to progress takes a will and courage that we must obtain and utilize with the guidance of wisdom. Where do we begin?

# 8 | The Other Side of the Crisis - The New Beginning

QUOTE:
"A NEW BEGINNING IS NOT STARTING OVER BUT GOD POSITIONING US IN A PLACE WE HAVE NEVER BEEN BEFORE TO GO TO WHERE WE HAVE NEVER BEEN BEFORE AND OBTAIN WHAT WE HAVE NEVER HAD BEFORE."
    APOSTLE H. KENNEDY MILLER

Principle:
"New beginnings come out of chaos or creativity; chose wisely which to use."
    Donald J. McClintock

**ISN'T IT ALWAYS** great to be on the other side of the crisis and then be able to look with 20/20 hind-sight and be relieved that the worst is over?

Being on the other side of the crisis brings about the steps of newness and rebuilding of life with thankfulness for surviving. Renewed hope inspires new energy to repair and replace that which was lost.

Wisdom is needed at this time to transition into the new beginning. It was this that Joseph both recognized and embraced. The business wheels of the economy had to be started again with urgency.

The people were given seed from the Joseph administration to begin the planting and restoring of the agricultural section of the economy. Animals would then be loaned for work in the fields. Twenty percent of everything harvested was to be collected for Pharaoh's storage and surplus.

This rebuilding of the main economy would once again replenish the market place by harvest time with the noise of commerce and negotiation, rather than the noise of hunger and anguish.

As the harvest came in from the first year after the famine stopped, the joy is in seeing crops grow in the field then returning to the satisfaction of life as normal. "Normal" is not what gets one through a crisis but rather what one intends to celebrate when a crisis is over.

The experience of going through something like this will change a person forever and a new "Normal" is attained.

It is this return to doing the things that make a people prosperous that reignite the flames of economic combustion. Along with the expansion of agriculture, jobs and businesses thrive once again.

Notice that the land is producing, the animals are working and multiplying, food is being sold, and the economy is growing again. Real Estate then becomes valuable again because it is a wealth producer.

When food and energy are in abundant supply at a reasonable cost, the economy flourishes. When energy is high priced, businesses slow down or raise prices. When food is too high priced, people will revolt. Joseph put workers to work, not continue government hand outs.

The welfare of the last seven years of famine ended. People had to get back to working the fields nd supplying a commodity to trade in business. Producers began producing again and the economy of Egypt grew.

The premise is to over produce with high productivity. It is then a nation has enough for its entire population and then can export trade to other nations. The truly wealthiest nations are those who do not have to meet the needs of their population by importing and borrowing but by exporting and lending.

The premise was to import the wealth of other nations, not import the things needed for daily survival. When a nation imports everything it needs, soon its wealth is paid out to those they trade with.

The true wealth of a nation is its people and the treasure they have to offer. Some may believe that a nation should train their workers only as far as necessary and then pay them an amount more than what will keep them from revolting and destroying all business and less than what will cause them to quit and stop working.

I believe that all should be given the power to attain all that they choose by the given fair rules of our Creator. Those that then choose unwisely end their life with a pittance. Those that choose wisely end their life in abundance with enough to pay for healthcare.

Once the economy was up and running, Joseph retired comfortably on personal wealth and a government pension. He retired at 44 years old financially independent and enjoyed his family. He may have still been a consultant to the governmental leadership. He lived to be 110 and healthcare costs did not eat up his fortune.

It is the immediate years following a crisis that are the most rewarding financially. One must be ready to reap those rewards. The best position to be in is optimizing the "spring back" from the bottom.

If you only survived, you would have to start all over again. If you were prepared, you would be postured to prosper from the upward thrust of prosperity.

# Epilogue

## Call to Action

**THIS LAST SECTION** is for different levels of social and economically levels; calling each to action. Individual, corporate, or governmental; this section is to provide you with both possible answers and points of action.

When there is a window of opportunity that is the time to take full advantage and ready one's self for the success of the future. One cannot afford to stand idly by and not produce any action. Inaction is the trap with in a trap. Action will only come when thinking has been transformed. Action is the proof of believing the probability of the future outcome is reasonable.

It is those who had the fortitude to prepare and act that position themselves for the best possible results. They have both outcomes covered. In this epilogue, I want to disclose to you the steps of action that will enable you to properly prepare and produce a portfolio that will be a life saver in the both scenarios of the times.

This plan of action will take courage and discipline.

It will require acquiring the knowledge and understanding necessary to adapt and tweak your plan to best fit your particular circumstances as they reflect to the contrast upon the canvas of economic conditions.

Enclosed below are several sections of steps to action for several levels of economic and power structure. Proper action befriends "Time" for future benefits.

## JOSEPH PLAN

**Survival-**
1 Water
   a Stored Supply
   b Filter & Decontaminate Tablets
   c Store Nature's Supply
2 Food
   a Stored Supply – long term storage, expiration dates longer than 1 year.
   b Garden Supply
   c Seed to Grow Supply
3 Shelter
   a Paid for & Secure
   b Protection from Elements and Outside Impact (Firearms)
   c Multi-Purpose
4 Energy
   a Batteries
   b Electric Generator – Gas or Propane, Manual
   c Grill – Propane or/and Charcoal, Wood
   d Matches and Lighters
   e Candles and/or Flashlights
5 Money
   a Gold – Wealth
   b Silver – Barter
   c U.S. Cash Money not Electronic for emergency transaction
   d Foreign Currency – Swiss Franc / or Aussie Dollar

- Currency that is from a nation not dependant on trade with US
6 Animals that Produce from Grass and Grain such as Chickens, Turkeys, Cows

## **Use Adversity for Opportunity**

1. MULTIPLE STREAMS of INCOME
   a. Internet based Business
   b. Home-based Business
   c. Turn-Key Multi-Marketing Business
      i. Financial Services
      ii. Survival Food Business
      iii. Water Purifier Business
      iv. Coupon Report Business
2. SAVING MONEY METHODS
   a. Coupon Shopping
   b. Conservation
   c. Synergy
   d. Sharing
3. MONEY for SURVIVAL & SAVING
   a. Cash
   b. Foreign Currency
   c. Silver & Precious Metal
4. ANNUITY with FINANCIAL FLOOR GUARANTEE
5. LAND purchases with Natural Resources
6. PAY OFF ALL DEBT
   a. Understand Leverage and Levels of Financial Solvency
7. HEALTH & WELLNESS NUTRITIONAL PLAN
   a. Super Foods–Anti-Oxidants, Anti-Inflammatory, Cancer fighters
8. UNDERSTANDING the MARKET, OPTIONS to BENEFIT from DOWNTURN
   a. Requires Financial Literacy

    b Requires Brokerage Account
9  LIVE ON SIMPLE BUDGET
    a Built in Savings Plan
    b Built in Spending Plan
    c Built in Giving Plan
10 RELATIONSHIPS
    a Build Partnership
    b Build Investment
    c Build Synergy
    d Build Ruler-ship

**Governmental Sector:** When there is an envelope of time prior to possible or certain hard times, one must utilize the Joseph principal. During that forward moving good year store 20% of all income. During a famine, base survival follows the necessities of life: food, water, and shelter. Ultimately food and water will reign as having the most value to life.

The storage of food is crucial when land production of food grows thin or is hard to produce. Once the crisis is over, food production (agriculture) would be next important to supply and resupply those necessities of life. Seed and land will be the hottest commodities.

These are the wealth of the land: "real estate, produce, livestock, wood, etc." In the Bible, silver was used in most land purchases and transactions. Brass was the lowest in value used in the purchase of daily use items and/or with barter. Gold was the king's wealth standard. These are the monies of the ages. When we are able to put aside 20% of our increase and then 20% of all income into the sustainable storage of durable assets, we preserve survival wealth. Assets can include silos for grain storage or assets that return value according to convertible trade. It is then that we have captured true intrinsic value especially if we own the land free and clear.

If times do get tough our lives will change. How we survival will change what we need to both prepare as wise children and press closer to God that His glory be made known. We must be wise as Joseph.

I am not against wealth, but I am against wealth without godly principles governing the hearts and behavior of those with great power over the lives of millions of people. We need more empowerment and partnership rather than basic employment.

*Deuteronomy 8 verses 11 to 20* state that when there is plenty and a bountiful supply, God warns against forgetting the Lord and his commands. It is not us but God who has given the power to get wealth. We utilize that power to harvest in wealth and harness those seasons of plenty and bountiful supply.

When people are satisfied and their belly is full, complacency comes and avarice springs up from the evil of thanklessness and irreverence.

It was evident by the wisdom of Joseph that he was clothed with something that others could not strip off of him nor cause him to abandon by hardship and cruel situations. He was carrying dreams in his spirit, excellence in his mind and protocol in his behavior. His integrity for the truth and to please his God was uncompromised.

Even though he suffered many hardships, Joseph had a distinction that became of destiny importance. Joseph was prepared to save two nations and his character was strong as iron and steel to hold up under the weight of adversity so that he could shoulder great responsibility.

We need great leaders today that have the attributes and characteristics of Joseph. It is sad to say that needing them and having them in charge are two totally different scenarios.

Economy- the first measurement for stating the health of the economy is usually GDP which stands for gross domestic product. It is the amount in dollars that the entire economy produces, spends, and/

or transacts, including the government. In truth, it is the speed of money being transacted for goods and services that gets counted as income or gross income.

When financial transactions begin to speed up, more money is needed to accommodate those transactions so that the system is not inadvertently slowed down waiting for money to clear hands and catch up with the transactions. This was the trouble that occurred when one could cash in their money for gold on the gold standard; there was the trouble of shipping and storing huge amount of gold for some to later be carrying around.

Acceleration of economy and inflation of money supply has many effects, one of these being a rubber band effect or bubble. When the economy is running smoothly, accelerating and expanding, there is

opportunity for bubbles to form and the rubber band to be extended beyond its elasticity capacity.

When the government invites legal operation of those whose ethical and moral standards are only governed by what the law clearly states, then sharks and piranhas are given permission to eat at the rubber band and pop the bubble. It is an injustice and a fraud that so many unaware, uneducated, and uninformed people are caught inside the rubber band and inside the bubble when it bursts. It is that recoiling and contraction that catches the unsuspecting masses in the crossfire causing much pain and financial loss. Many times this leads to an economic recession.

One would think that any representative or elected official with half a brain for finances or having any educational understanding of how business and the economy works would know to develop laws and policies that safeguard the masses from these unfortunate happenings. Yes, the government cannot take away the entire risk of transacting business, but it can level the playing field so that fairness and justice prevail.

I highly recommend financial education classes for all individuals prior to certain financial contracts with agreements in order that those entering into major transactions such as: mortgages, stocks, bonds and derivatives are both illuminated and totally informed of the costs, rewards, and dangers prior to such transactions. Those that have the knowledge could not defraud those that are uneducated and influence an unfair advantage.

Furthermore it should be required that all elected officials and judges be financially educated if serving in a capacity or judgments, laws, and/or policies that could be written or made law. All of which have a financial impact upon the lives of those they govern. In other words, you don't serve in a place because of political advantage without having or being armed with the proper knowledge and education.

Thusly, each and every elected official trained and certified would or could be held accountable, liable and/or criminally charged if perpetrating a fraud, misrepresentation, or cronyism benefits at the cost and despair of the people of the nation.

While sitting in finance class something that Dr. Chang said caused a stirring of thought in my mind. He said that the accounting balance sheet is not conducive to the market value in good times and the market balance sheet was not viable in the volatile times. This caused me to think about a measure taking into account the accounting balance sheet or book value as the base and the market financial balance sheet as expander.

A new creative formula that brings a weighted balance between the cycles like beta, but with the accounting balance sheet injected into the equation. This would establish an average or mean from which the market financial sheet would become the deviation from the mean. Then one would use Bollinger bands to set standard deviations for the highest indicators. Not on a 20, 30, 100 or 200 day moving average but on the overlay of six months which is the two quarters necessary to predict a recession then a one year three year and five-year cycles. Given this hypothesis there would be a base monetary book value as a foundation of valuing a company and show the extent of their leverage.

During the housing bubble crisis, it was the inability to pay or maintain cash flow that killed the underlying derivatives. That led to the inability to value the mortgage backed securities. There was no tie to an asset, only the ability to repay. Clearly the peak was achieved in 2006 but the lag time into 2008 set the course for housing resale values to plummet to zero. Rules caused lenders to carry those values of their books although the property itself has intrinsic value.

When nobody is buying then what is it worth? This has to be answered because of true value. What is the resale and what is the rebuilt price minus depreciation?

The concrete, wood, windows, siding, etc. are worth something even if no one wants to buy because of the market prices of the goods and services it would take to rebuild. Yes, without someone wanting to buy it, its value would decline over time without proper maintenance and upkeep.

If we tied property values to the year that crossed the 20 year mean by declaring it to be the standard base value; overvalued properties would be quickly seen as a risk not merely what the market can bear. It will have equilibrium; as high as it goes is as deep as it will go. There seems to be about a 20 year boom to bust recovery cycle to the American dream of owning a house.

How much wealth has been produced when balanced to inflation and the decline of currency value?

Given that taxes are punitive in nature and in their own right beyond the common patriotic duty to a nation's coffers for the basic necessities of protection, proper government operations, infrastructure and crime prevention/punishment, taxes must be utilized with great wisdom. How that a government uses the taxing system will impact and have bearing on the behavior of the majority. Since politicians have learned that taxes are not only punishment, but steer behavior to the most part except for those things that cannot be controlled by monetary means, they use this politically to advance their philosophical agenda. The great problem that the nation is facing is entitlement expansion.

As the government/citizen partnership has led to

something for nothing or too much for something; also the private sector has turned to maximizing profits and value for shareholders. Neglecting to partner with those who do the work in an educated way, we have launched our nation down an unsustainable path. We are given extra long unemployment benefits. Instead of help, it has become an incentive to stay unemployed.

Yes, we should help those that cannot survive without the help of others, but too many are milking the system for all it is worth while doing nothing in return or value. Taxes above 20% can become huge burden upon the system and economy forcing distortion, pushing prices higher and can lead to an economic slowdown: recession- a steady or slowly gradual adjustment system is best.

**Real viable possible answers:**

1. Financial education in investments and mortgages should be made available to all workers and a literacy test passed in order to attain a mortgage.
2. Risk shared mortgage-backed securities-banks and originators keep some skin in the game and cannot foreclose on a cash flow home equal to interest +$10 equity due to hardship loss of job, illness, injury or interest spiked changes payment increases that cannot exceed 5% of the previous payment.
3. A corporate tax rate of 27% to those higher percentage of workforce increase; 20% for all small businesses: corporate (C, S etc.), partnerships or sole partner and increase workforce

by retaining percentage of workers tenure locked with duly domestic workforce who are legal citizens.
4. Tax code reform, everybody pays something – no free rides.
5. Subsidies should be pro-growth and expansion not protected to limit.
6. Energy policy should be one of clean environment yet friendly to all out production of all types of energy.
7. Corporate and business partnership with workers such as profit-sharing as part of employer benefits paid out partly to retirement assets accounts. Corporate salaries and benefits at the top cannot exceed 5 to 10 times the average pay of all workers. Including 20% tax on producers in good times, and 0% in bad times, 20% during recovery.
8. Triples the tax on all tobacco and alcohol (above the proof level of wine) tiered in three segments. Luxury is taxed at highest levels.
9. Revenue by growth in transaction's speeding money into the coffers while maintaining due restraints on spending.
10. Raise the age of Social Security full benefits to 70 years, and deduct Social Security tax out without ceiling levels. Top 1% will waive rights to receive Social Security benefits at retirement with a 1% refund of all Social Security taxes that they paid in over the course of their working years.

It is time for "The Joseph Principle" to be enacted in our lives. Write out your plan with goals and steps of action. The challenge is not just for our elected officials; rather it is for all to engage in the essential ingredients that will produce a viable and sustainable economic future.

# References Recommended

The Holy Bible,

# Bibliography

Berman, Jillian. "Huff Post Business "75 Percent of Americans Don't Have Enough SAvings to Cover Their Bills For Six Months: Survey"." 24 6 2013. <u>The Huffington Post.</u> 21 8 2013 <www.huffingtonpost.com/2013/06/24/americans-savings_n_3478932.html>.

Crutsinger, Martin. "Huff Post Business "Federal Reserve to Keep Buying &85 Billion in Bonds Each Month Until Job Market Improves"." 19 6 2013. <u>The Huffington Post.</u> 21 8 2013 <www.huffingtonpost.com/2013/06/19/federal-reserve-bond-buying_n_3467097.html>.

"Economic News Release." 2 8 2013. <u>Bureau of Labor Statistics.</u> 21 8 2013 <www.bls.gov/news.releases/empsit.t15.htm>.

"Mortgage Debt Outstanding." 6 2013. <u>Board of Governors of the Federal Reserve.</u> 21 8 2013 <www.federalreserve.gov/econresdata/releases/mortoutstand/current.html>.

"Reports - The Debt to the Penny and Who Holds

It." 21 8 2013. Treasury Direct. 21 8 2013 <www.treasurydirect.gov/NP/debt?current>.

"US Debt Clock. org." 21 8 2013. United States Government. 21 8 2013 <www.usdebtclock.org>.

# Advertisements & Products

### Kingdom Financial Institute, CD Sessions in Binder

13 Sessions for Financial Literacy

Subjects Include: Credit Repair, Budgeting, Mortgages, Rental Property, Business Formation, Wealth Strategies, Intellectual Property, the Millionaire Mindset, & Investments.

### Getting the Rocks Right, CD Messages in Binder

Series set for Personal Development & Abundance Acceleration

Subjects Include: Spiritual Foundation, Order, Action, Expectancy, Preparedness, Breakthrough, & Acceleration.

# Contact Information

Donald J. McClintock
e-mail: djmcclintock62@gmail.com
website: www.outskirtspress.com/Joseph_Principle

# Author's Short Biography

Don McClintock was thrust into the financial field after being named "Trustee" for a minor's estate. Since 1995, Don has been licensed in life insurance. He received his securities license and worked as a financial analyst since 1996 while ministering at Eagle Heights Worship Center as Senior Pastor since 1998.

Don is presently attending Missouri State University majoring in Finance with two minors, Economics and Entrepreneurship. He presently manages accounts for clients totaling over $1.5 million.

Don has been full-time in ministry since 1986 and his ministry experience includes: youth ministry (5 years), evangelism to 101 churches in 17 states (7 years), and pastoral leadership (15 years).

He has developed a financial education seminar called "Kingdom Financial Institute." This was designed to educate the working public in a wide range of financial matters.

He has written papers concerning "The Economic Crisis of 2008 – Reasons for Recession" and "The Economy is in Crisis."

Don has been married to his soul partner and wife, Brenda, since 1989. They have three children, Crystal, David, and Brittany. They have lived in Springfield, Missouri since April of 1991.

CPSIA information can be obtained at www.ICGtesting.com
Printed in the USA
LVOW06s0543031214

416656LV00001B/29/P